Presidents of the United States

**Practice Cursive Handwriting
with Quotes from U.S. Presidents**

Classic Copywork: Cursive   **Vol. 4**

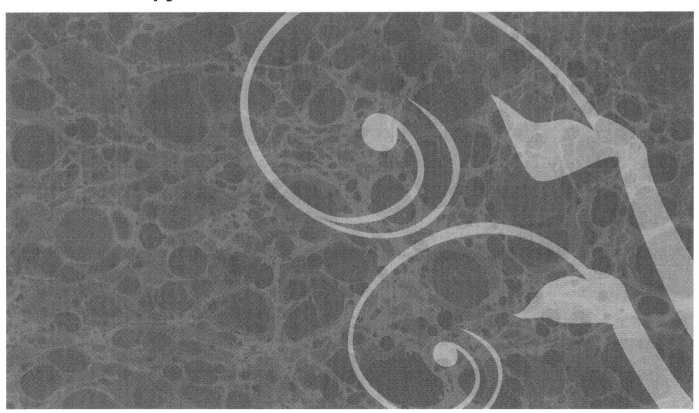

ISBN: 0692636579
ISBN-13: 978-0692636572

Table of Contents

George Washington

The 1st President of the United States

*I hope I shall possess firmness and virtue
enough to maintain what I consider the most
enviable of all titles, the character of an honest man.*

I hope I shall possess firmness and virtue

enough to maintain what I consider the

most enviable of all titles, the character

of an honest man.

George Washington,

The First President of the United States

John Adams

The 2nd President of the United States

*Facts are stubborn things; and whatever
may be our wishes, our inclinations,
or the dictates of our passion,
they cannot alter the state of facts and evidence.*

Facts are stubborn things; and whatever may

be our wishes, our inclinations, or the dictates

of our passion, they cannot alter the state

of facts and evidence.

John Adams,

The Second President of the United States

Thomas Jefferson

The 3rd President of the United States

I hold it that a little rebellion now and then is a good thing,
and as necessary in the political world as storms in the physical.

I hold it that a little rebellion now and then is a

good thing, and as necessary in the political world

as storms in the physical.

Thomas Jefferson,

The Third President of the United States

James Madison
The 4th President of the United States

Religion and government will both exist in greater purity, the less they are mixed together.

Religion and government will both exist in

greater purity, the less they are mixed together.

James Madison,

The Fourth President of the United States

James Monroe
The 5th President of the United States

If we look to the history of other nations,
ancient or modern, we find no example
of a growth so rapid, so gigantic,
of a people so prosperous and happy.

If we look to the history of other nations,

ancient or modern, we find no example

of a growth so rapid, so gigantic,

of a people so prosperous and happy.

James Monroe,

The Fifth President of the United States

John Quincy Adams

The 6th President of the United States

If your actions inspire others to dream more, learn more, do more and become more, you are a leader.

If your actions inspire others to dream more, learn

more, do more and become more, you are a leader.

John Quincy Adams,

The Sixth President of the United States

Andrew Jackson

The 7th President of the United States

Any man worth his salt will stick up for what he believes right, but it takes a slightly better man to acknowledge instantly and without reservation that he is in error.

Any man worth his salt will stick up for what he

believes right, but it takes a slightly better man to

acknowledge instantly and without reservation

that he is in error.

Andrew Jackson,

The Seventh President of the United States

Martin Van Buren

The 8th President of the United States

The government should not be guided by temporary excitement, but by sober second thought.

The government should not be guided by

temporary excitement, but by sober second thought.

Martin Van Buren,

The Eighth President of the United States

William Henry Harrison

The 9th President of the United States

The only legitimate right to govern is an express grant of power from the governed.

The only legitimate right to govern is an express

grant of power from the governed.

William Henry Harrison,

The Ninth President of the United States

John Tyler

The 10th President of the United States

Wealth can only be accumulated by the earnings of industry and the savings of frugality.

Wealth can only be accumulated by the earnings

of industry and the savings of frugality.

John Tyler,

The Tenth President of the United States

James Polk

The 11th President of the United States

*One great object of the Constitution was
to restrain majorities from oppressing
minorities or encroaching upon their just rights.*

One great object of the Constitution was to restrain

majorities from oppressing minorities or

encroaching upon their just rights.

James Polk,

The Eleventh President of the United States

Zachary Taylor

The 12th President of the United States

In the discharge of duties my guide will be the Constitution, which I this day swear to preserve, protect, and defend.

In the discharge of duties my guide will be the

Constitution, which I this day swear to preserve,

protect, and defend.

Zachary Taylor,

The Twelfth President of the United States

Millard Fillmore

The 13th President of the United States

Let us remember that revolutions do not always establish freedom. Our own free institutions were not the offspring of our revolution. They existed before.

Let us remember that revolutions do not always

establish freedom. Our own free institutions were not

the offspring of our revolution. They existed before.

Millard Fillmore,

The Thirteenth President of the United States

Franklin Pierce

The 14th President of the United States

The dangers of a concentration of all power in the general government of a confederacy so vast as ours are too obvious to be disregarded.

The dangers of a concentration of all power in the

general government of a confederacy so vast as ours

are too obvious to be disregarded.

Franklin Pierce,

The Fourteenth President of the United States

James Buchanan
The 15th President of the United States

Liberty must be allowed to work out its natural results; and these will, ere long, astonish the world.

Liberty must be allowed to work out its natural

results; and these will, ere long, astonish the world.

James Buchanan,

The Fifteenth President of the United States

Abraham Lincoln
The 16th President of the United States

*Four score and seven years ago
our fathers brought forth on this continent,
a new nation, conceived in liberty,
and dedicated to the proposition
that all men are created equal.*

Four score and seven years ago our fathers brought

forth on this continent a new nation, conceived

in liberty, and dedicated to the proposition that all

men are created equal.

Abraham Lincoln,

The Sixteenth President of the United States

Andrew Johnson

The 17th President of the United States

*Who, then, will govern? The answer must be
Man—for we have no angels in the shape of men,
as yet, who are willing to take charge of our political affairs.*

Who, then, will govern? The answer must be

Man - for we have no angels in the shape of men,

as yet, who are willing to take charge of our

political affairs.

Andrew Johnson,

The Seventeenth President of the United States

Ulysses S. Grant

The 18th President of the United States

The art of war is simple enough.
Find out where your enemy is.
Get at him as soon as you can.
Strike him as hard as you can,
and keep moving on.

The art of war is simple enough.

Find out where your enemy is.

Get at him as soon as you can.

Strike him as hard as you can,

and keep moving on.

Ulysses S. Grant,

The Eighteenth President of the United States

Rutherford B. Hayes

The 19th President of the United States

As knowledge spreads, wealth spreads.
To diffuse knowledge is to diffuse wealth.
To give all an equal chance to acquire knowledge
is the best and surest way to give all
an equal chance to acquire property.

As knowledge spreads, wealth spreads.

To diffuse knowledge is to diffuse wealth.

To give all an equalchance to acquire knowledge

is the best and surest way to give all an equal

chance to acquire property.

Rutherford B. Hayes,

The Nineteenth President of the United States

James A. Garfield

The 20th President of the United States

Be fit for more than the thing you are now doing.
Let everyone know that you have a reserve in yourself;
that you have more power than you are now using.
If you are not too large for the place you occupy,
you are too small for it.

Be fit for more than the thing you are now doing.

Let everyone know that you have a reserve in

yourself; that you have more power than you are

now using. If you are not too large for the place

you occupy, you are too small for it.

James A. Garfield,

The Twentieth President of the United States

Chester A. Arthur

The 21st President of the United States

*The extravagant expenditure of public money
is an evil not to be measured by the value of that
money to the people who are taxed for it.*

The extravagant expenditure of public money is

an evil not to be measured by the value of that

money to the people who are taxed for it.

Chester A. Arthur,

The Twenty-first President of the United States

Grover Cleveland

The 22nd and the 24th President of the United States

*A truly American sentiment recognizes the dignity
of labor and the fact that honor lies in honest toil.
Contented labor is an element of national prosperity.*

A truly American sentiment recognizes

the dignity of labor and the fact that

honor lies in honest toil. Contented labor

is an element of national prosperity.

Grover Cleveland,

The Twenty-second and the Twenty-fourth

President of the United States

Benjamin Harrison

The 23rd President of the United States

I pity the man who wants a coat so cheap that the man or woman who produces the cloth or shapes it into a garment will starve in the process.

I pity the man who wants a coat so cheap that the

man or woman who produces the cloth or shapes it

into a garment will starve in the process.

Benjamin Harrison,

The Twenty-third President of the United States

William McKinley
The 25th President of the United States

Let us ever remember that our interest is in concord, not in conflict; and that our real eminence rests in the victories of peace, not those of war.

Let us ever remember that our interest is in

concord, not in conflict; and that our real

eminence rests in the victories of peace,

not those of war.

William McKinley,

The Twenty-fifth President of the United States

Theodore Roosevelt
The 26th President of the United States

It is not the critic who counts; not the man who points out how the strong man stumbles, or where the doer of deeds could have done them better. The credit belongs to the man who is actually in the arena, whose face is marred by dust and sweat and blood; who strives valiantly; who errs, who comes short again and again, because there is no effort without error and shortcoming; but who does actually strive to do the deeds; who knows great enthusiasms, the great devotions; who spends himself in a worthy cause; who at the best knows in the end the triumph of high achievement, and who at the worst, if he fails, at least fails while daring greatly, so that his place shall never be with those cold and timid souls who neither know victory nor defeat.

It is not the critic who counts; not the man who

points out how the strong man stumbles, or where

the doer of deeds could have done them better. The

credit belongs to the man who is actually in the

arena, whose face is marred by dust and sweat and

blood; who strives valiantly; who errs, who comes

short again and again, because there is no effort

without error and shortcoming; but who does

actually strive to do the deeds; who knows great

enthusiasms, the great devotions; who spends

himself in a worthy cause; who at the best

knows in the end the triumph of high

achievement, and who at the worst, if he fails,

at least fails while daring greatly, so that his

place shall never be with those cold and timid

souls who neither know victory nor defeat.

Theodore Roosevelt,

The Twenty-sixth President of the United States

William Howard Taft

The 27th President of the United States

Next to the right of liberty, the right of property is the most important individual right guaranteed by the Constitution and the one which, united with that of personal liberty, has contributed more to the growth of civilization than any other institution established by the human race.

Next to the right of liberty, the right of property is

the most important individual right guaranteed by

the Constitution and the one which, united with

that of personal liberty, has contributed more to the

growth of civilization than any other institution

established by the human race.

William Howard Taft,

The Twenty-seventh President of the United States

Woodrow Wilson

The 28th President of the United States

We grow great by dreams. All big men are dreamers.
They see things in the soft haze of a spring day
or in the red fire of a winter's night.
Some of us let these dreams die,
but others nourish and protect them;
nurse them through bad days till they come true.

We grow great by dreams. All big men are

dreamers. They see things in the soft haze of a

spring day or in the red fire of a winter's night.

Some of us let these dreams die, but others nourish

and protect them; nurse them through bad days

till they come true.

Woodrow Wilson,

The Twenty-eighth President of the United States

Warren G. Harding

The 29th President of the United States

Our most dangerous tendency is to expect too much of government, and at the same time do for it too little.

Our most dangerous tendency is to expect too much

of government, and at the same time do for it

too little.

Warren G. Harding,

The Twenty-ninth President of the United States

Calvin Coolidge

The 30th President of the United States

America is a large country.
It is a tolerant country.
It has room within its borders
for many races and many creeds.

America is a large country. It is a tolerant

country. It has room within its borders

for many races and many creeds.

Calvin Coolidge,

The Thirtieth President of the United States

Herbert Hoover

The 31st President of the United States

Whatever doubt there may be as to the quality or purpose of our free speech we certainly have ample volumes in production.

Whatever doubt there may be as to the quality or

purpose of our free speech we certainly have ample

volumes in production.

Herbert Hoover,

The Thirty-first President of the United States

Franklin D. Roosevelt

The 32nd President of the United States

Let us not be afraid to help each other—let us never forget that government is ourselves and not an alien power over us. The ultimate rulers of our democracy are not a President and Senators and Congressmen and Government officials but the voters of this country.

Let us not be afraid to help each other — let us

never forget that government is ourselves and

not an alien power over us. The ultimate rulers

of our democracy are not a President and

Senators and Congressmen and Government

officials but the voters of this country.

Franklin D. Roosevelt,

The Thirty-second President of the United States

Harry S. Truman

The 33rd President of the United States

In reading the lives of great men, I found that the first victory they won was over themselves... self-discipline with all of them came first.

In reading the lives of great men, I found that

the first victory they won was over themselves...

self-discipline with all of them came first.

Harry S. Truman,

The Thirty-third President of the United States

Dwight D. Eisenhower

The 34th President of the United States

I hate war as only a soldier who has lived it can, only as one who has seen its brutality, its stupidity.

I hate war as only a soldier who has lived it can,

only as one who has seen its brutality,

its stupidity.

Dwight D. Eisenhower,

The Thirty-fourth President of the United States

John F. Kennedy

The 35th President of the United States

The energy, the faith, the devotion which we bring to this endeavor will light our country and all who serve it—and the glow from that fire can truly light the world. And so, my fellow Americans: ask not what your country can do for you—ask what you can do for your country.

The energy, the faith, the devotion which we bring

to this endeavor will light our country and all who

serve it — and the glow from that fire can truly

light the world. And so, my fellow Americans:

ask not what your country can do for you — ask

what you can do for your country.

John F. Kennedy,

The Thirty-fifth President of the United States

Lyndon B. Johnson
The 36th President of the United States

Justice requires us to remember that when any citizen denies his fellow, saying, "His color is not mine," or "His beliefs are strange and different," in that moment he betrays America, though his forebears created this nation.

Justice requires us to remember that when any

citizen denies his fellow, saying, "His color is not

mine," or "His beliefs are strange and different,"

in that moment he betrays America,

though his forebears created this nation.

Lyndon B. Johnson,

The Thirty-sixth President of the United States

Richard Nixon

The 37th President of the United States

*Any nation that decides the only way to
achieve peace is through peaceful means
is a nation that will soon be a piece of another nation.*

Any nation that decides the only way to achieve

peace is through peaceful means is a nation that

will soon be a piece of another nation.

Richard Nixon,

The Thirty-seventh President of the United States

Gerald Ford

The 38th President of the United States

As we continue our American adventure…all our heroes and heroines of war and peace send us this single, urgent message: though prosperity is a good thing, though compassionate charity is a good thing, though institutional reform is a good thing, a nation survives only so long as the spirit of sacrifice and self-discipline is strong within its people. Independence has to be defended as well as declared; freedom is always worth fighting for; and liberty ultimately belongs only to those willing to suffer for it.

As we continue our American adventure ... all our

heroes and heroines of war and peace send us this

single, urgent message: though prosperity is a good

thing, though compassionate charity is a good

thing, though institutional reform is a good thing,

a nation survives only so long as the spirit of

sacrifice and self-discipline is strong within its

people. Independence has to be defended as well as

declared; freedom is always worth fighting for; and

liberty ultimately belongs only to those willing

to suffer for it.

Gerald Ford,

The Thirty-eighth President of the United States

Jimmy Carter

The 39th President of the United States

America did not invent human rights.
In a very real sense, it is the other way round.
Human rights invented America.
Ours was the first nation in the history of the
world to be founded explicitly on such an idea.

America did not invent human rights. In a very

real sense, it is the other way round. Human rights

invented America. Ours was the first nation in the

history of the world to be founded explicitly on

such an idea.

Jimmy Carter,

The Thirty-ninth President of the United States

Ronald Reagan

The 40th President of the United States

The nine most terrifying words in the English language are: I'm from the Government, and I'm here to help.

The nine most terrifying words in the English

language are: I'm from the Government,

and I'm here to help.

Ronald Reagan,

The Fortieth President of the United States

George H. W. Bush
The 41st President of the United States

I do not like broccoli and I haven't liked it since I was a little kid and my mother made me eat it. And I'm President of the United States and I'm not going to eat any more broccoli.

I do not like broccoli and I haven't liked it since

I was a little kid and my mother made me eat it.

And I'm President of the United States and I'm

not going to eat any more broccoli.

George H. W. Bush,

The Forty-first President of the United States

Bill Clinton
The 42nd President of the United States

Our democracy must be not only the envy of the world but the engine of our own renewal. There is nothing wrong with America that cannot be cured by what is right with America.

Our democracy must be not only the envy of the

world but the engine of our own renewal. There is

nothing wrong with America that cannot be cured

by what is right with America.

Bill Clinton,

The Forty-second President of the United States

George W. Bush

The 43rd President of the United States

The peaceful transfer of authority is rare in history,
yet common in our country. With a simple oath,
we affirm old traditions and make new beginnings.

The peaceful transfer of authority is rare in history,

yet common in our country.

With a simple oath, we affirm old traditions

and make new beginnings.

George W. Bush,

The Forty-third President of the United States

Barack Obama
The 44th President of the United States

First and foremost, let us remember that change has never been quick. Change has never been simple, or without controversy. Change depends on persistence. Change requires determination.

First and foremost, let us remember that change has

never been quick. Change has never been simple, or

without controversy. Change depends on persistence.

Change requires determination.

Barack Obama,

The Forty-fourth President of the United States

Want More?

Great Literature Cursive Copywork

Practice Handwriting with Excerpts from the Great Books

Experience some of the great moments in classic literature and history while improving your cursive handwriting. Copywork is the best way to learn basic grammar, spelling, and composition skills, so why practice penmanship with random words and sentences when you could be exploring amazing stories and poems by authors including:

Shakespeare	*Abraham Lincoln*
Homer	*Jane Austen*
Aristotle	*James Joyce*
Robert Frost	*Robert Louis Stevenson*
Mark Twain	*Rudyard Kipling*
Edgar Allen Poe	*...and many more*

This book includes over 40 passages. Buy online at www.speset.com.

Want More?

Inspirational Quotes Copywork

Practice Handwriting with Inspirational Quotes from Great Leaders

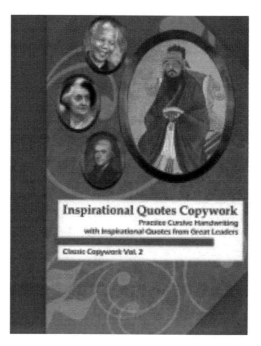

Learn from the wit and wisdom of some of the greatest leaders, inventors, writers, and thinkers throughout history while improving your cursive handwriting. Copywork is the best way to learn basic grammar, spelling, and composition skills, so why practice penmanship with random words and sentences when you could be inspired by quotes about the value of hard work, education, persistence, optimism, courage, kindness, and many other virtues, in the actual words of great men and women, including:

Plato
Confucius
Mother Teresa
Nelson Mandela
Sun Tzu
Thomas Jefferson

Winston Churchill
Indira Ghandi
Abraham Lincoln
the Dalai Lama
Albert Einstein
…and many more

This book includes over 30 passages. Buy online at www.speset.com.

Looking for Print?

Classic Children's Literature

Practice Handwriting with Excerpts from Classic Children's Books

Explore favorite passages from some of the most-loved children's books while improving your handwriting skills. Copywork is the best way to learn basic grammar, spelling, and composition so why practice penmanship with random words and sentences when you could be enjoying excerpts from amazing stories including:

The Wizard of Oz
Alice in Wonderland
20,000 Leagues Under the Sea
Treasure Island
The Hobbit
Swiss Family Robinson

Pippi Longstocking
The Little Prince
Charlotte's Web
Winnie the Pooh
Peter Pan
…and many more

This book includes over 30 passages. Buy online at www.speset.com.

Made in the USA
Lexington, KY
10 August 2019